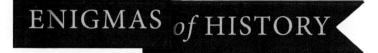

ENIGMAS *of* HISTORY

REVEALING THE SECRETS OF DINOSAURS

WORLD BOOK

a Scott Fetzer company
Chicago
www.worldbook.com

World Book edition of "Enigmas de la historia" by Editorial Sol 90.

Enigmas de la historia
Los últimos dinosaurios

This edition licensed from Editorial Sol 90 S.L.
Copyright 2013 Editorial Sol S.L. All rights reserved.

Revised printing, 2016
English-language revised edition copyright 2015
World Book, Inc.
Enigmas of History
Revealing the Secrets of Dinosaurs

World Book, Inc.
180 North LaSalle Street
Suite 900
Chicago, Illinois 60601
USA

For information about other World Book publications,
visit our website at **www.worldbook.com** or call
1-800-967-5325.

Library of Congress Cataloging-in-Publication Data

Los últimos dinosaurios. English
  Revealing the secrets of dinosaurs. -- English-language
revised edition.
     pages cm. -- (Enigmas of history)
  Summary: "An exploration of the questions and
mysteries surrounding the dinosaurs. Features include
a map, fact boxes, biographies of paleontologists and
famous experts on dinosaurs, places to see and visit,
a glossary, further readings, and index"-- Provided by
publisher.
  Includes index.
  ISBN 978-0-7166-2673-2
  1. Dinosaurs--Juvenile literature. I. World Book, Inc.
II. Series: Enigmas of history.
  QE861.5.R48 2015
  567.9--dc23
                                  2015009311

Enigmas of History Set ISBN: 978-0-7166-2670-1

Printed in China by Shenzhen Donnelley
Printing Co., Ltd., Guangdong Province
2nd printing June 2016

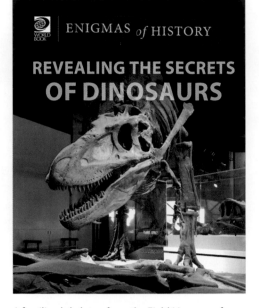

A fossilized skeleton from the Field Museum of
Chicago of a *Daspletosaurus,* a small tyrannosaur
of about 20 to 30 feet (8 to 9 meters) in length.
Tyrannosaurus rex is the largest, but there are at least
10 other species of tyrannosaur known to scientists.

© Don Di Sante

Staff

Glossary There is a glossary of terms on page 44. Terms defined in the glossary are in boldface **(type that looks like this)** on their first appearance on any *spread* (two facing pages). Words that are difficult to say are followed by a pronunciation (pruh NUHN see AY shuhn) the first time they are mentioned.

Contents

A genus is a scientific group of living or once-living things. A genus contains one or more closely related **species**. All genus names—such as *Allosaurus, Stegosaurus,* and *Triceratops*—are capitalized and italicized.

Secrets in the Bones

Dinosaurs lived and died more than 65 million years ago. Nobody today has ever seen a living dinosaur, yet virtually everyone knows what they are. Dinosaurs appear in video games, books, and movies. They are on t-shirts and lunch-boxes. How do we know what these **prehistoric** creatures looked like? What dinosaur secrets remain to be revealed?

People began to piece together the story of dinosaurs about 200 years ago. They did this—literally—by assembling *fossilized* (preserved remains from long ago) dinosaur bones that they found in the ground.

The fossils were the remains of animal bodies buried beneath layers of mud and sand millions of years ago. Over time, water and minerals seeped into tiny hollow spaces in the bones. Eventually, more layers of soil created enough pressure to change the soil in and around the bones to rock. The fossilized bones lay hidden as the land above them rose and fell and changed. Finally, people rediscovered some of the fossils, a sort of *prehistoric* (from long-ago time before written history) buried treasure.

How can anyone tell what an animal looked like from old bones or the im-print of an ancient footstep? It's not easy. Some people who found dinosaur bones in the past thought they came from ordinary animals. If the bones were really big, they might guess the animal had been an elephant or a whale. Sometimes they made up stories of giants or dragons.

During the 1800's, scientists began carefully comparing dinosaur bones with the skeletons of familiar modern and living animals. They thought the dino-saur bones belonged to *reptiles* (animals with lungs that hatch from shells), yet the skeletons were not quite the same as any reptile still alive. Modern reptiles, such as **crocodiles** and lizards, are scaly-skinned animals that lay hard-shelled eggs. The British scientist Sir Richard Owen (1804-1892) called the new group of prehistoric animals *Dinosauria,* from Latin words that meant *terribly great lizards.* As it turns out, dinosaurs were not actually a type of lizard, but the name stuck.

Scientists also studied the rocks in which they found the strange bones. This revealed that dinosaurs all lived during a period in Earth's history called the **Mesozoic Era** (from about 250 million to 65 million years ago). Scientists divide it into three periods—the *Triassic Period* (about 250 million to 200 million years ago), the **Jurassic Period** (about 200 million to 145 million years ago), and the **Cretaceous Period** (about 145 million to 65 million years ago). Dinosaur fossils first appear in rock from about 230 million years ago, during the Triassic Period. Dinosaurs ruled Earth as the dominant animals for about 160 million years. Then, at the end of the Cretaceous Period, they simply disappeared. Nobody knows why. There are some strong theories, but exact events remain mysterious.

Today's scientists continue the quest to discover more about dinosaurs. They use computer analysis and other technology to help solve the puzzle of what dinosaurs looked like and how they lived. However, the main puzzle pieces are still **fossil** and rock. These pieces are scattered across every continent, even Antarctica. The pieces themselves are often puzzles within the larger puzzle. Fossilized fragments must be analyzed and assembled to unlock their secrets.

Every year, scientists and amateur fossil hunters discover more dinosaur fossils. Scientists are still identifying new kinds of dinosaurs. They are learning about how dinosaurs lived. They are working out how dinosaurs are related to other types of reptiles and to other types of animals, especially birds. Who knows where the next big find will happen or what long hidden secrets are on the verge of being revealed!

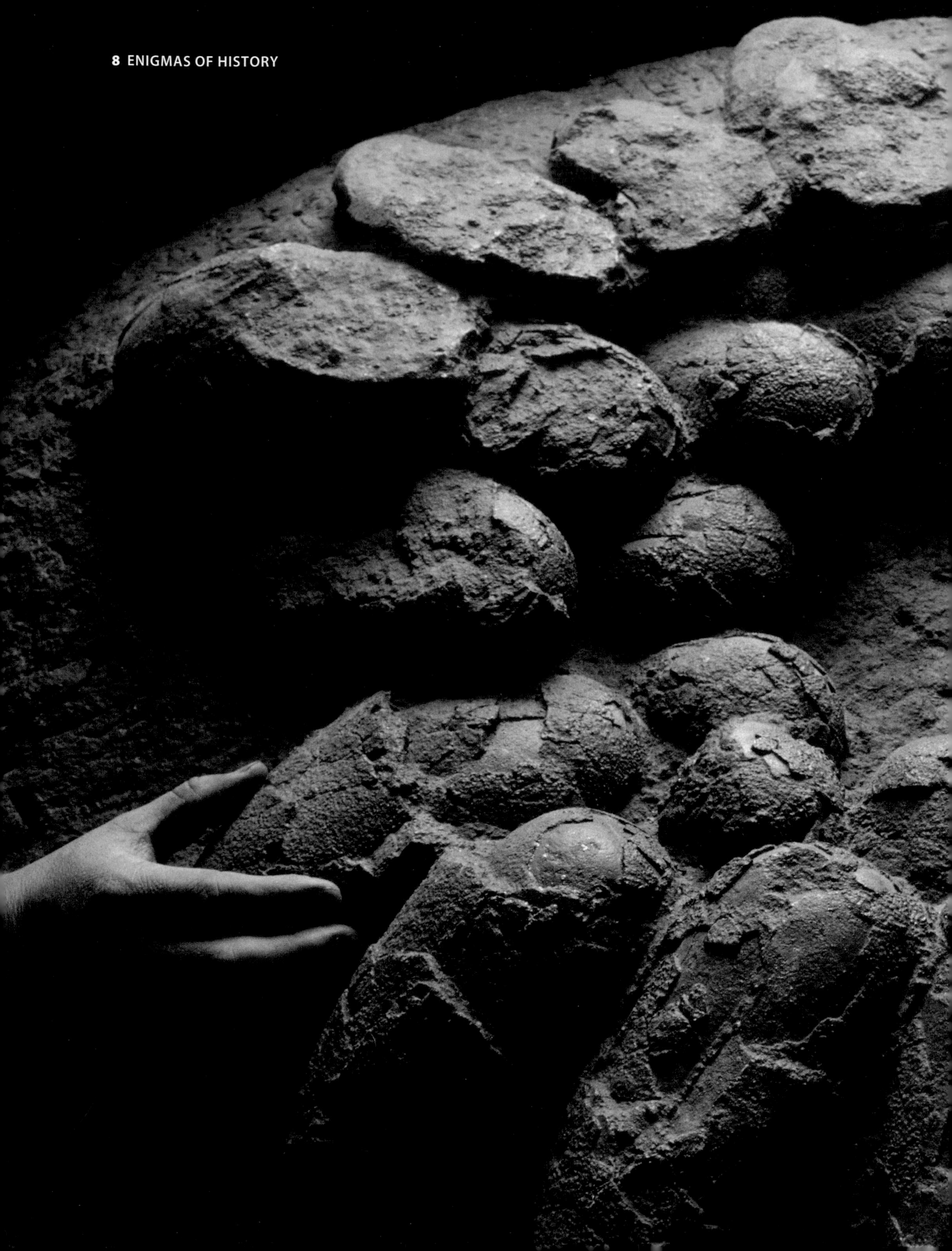

EGGS

A nest of **fossilized** dinosaur eggs found in Asia's windswept Gobi Desert reveals that even the eggs of some dinosaurs were big.

Dinosaurs: Beasts from Prehistory

Since the discovery of the remains of dinosaurs in the early 1800's, these prehistoric animals have fascinated people the world over. Scientists have managed to unlock some of the mysteries hidden in the fossilized bones of dinosaurs, but there is still much to discover.

Science began to reveal the mysteries surrounding dinosaurs about 200 years ago. The quest began with the discovery in Stonesfield, in the United Kingdom, of what appeared to be a large **fossilized** jaw containing several sharp teeth. The English churchman and **geologist** William Buckland (1784-1856) studied the fossil. In 1824, on becoming president of the Geological Society of London, Buckland announced the discovery of the previously unknown animal, which he named *Megalosaurus,* (mehg uh loh SAWR uhs), meaning *great lizard.* Later that year, he wrote the first complete description of a dinosaur. No one had ever named a dinosaur before. In fact, the word *dinosaur* had not yet been invented.

READING THE BONES
Meanwhile, in France, Baron Georges Cuvier (1769-1832) was doing pioneering work that would help scientists interpret the information hidden in fossils. Cuvier developed the study of comparative **anatomy**, a branch of science that compares the similarities and differences in the body structures of different kinds of animals. He examined living creatures and the remains of **prehistoric** animals, leading him to become known as the father of both comparative anatomy and **paleontology.** *Paleontology* (PAY lee on TOL uh jee) is the study of animals, plants, and other organisms that lived in prehistoric times.

In 1817, Cuvier published *The Animal Kingdom,* in which he classified animals into four groups—vertebrates, mollusks, articulates, and radiates—based on the nature and arrangement of their organs and body systems. He also proposed a principle he called the *correlation of parts.* The principle said the structure and function of all the parts in an animal's body were related to and resulted from the animal's interaction with its environment. For example, an animal that ate only plants would have teeth suited for eating plants, not for tearing meat. All the other parts of the animal's body would be similarly suited to the life of a plant-eater. Cuvier used his principle to reconstruct complete skeletons of prehistoric animals based on a limited number of fossilized bones.

TRICERATOPS

One of the most recognizable dinosaurs, *Triceratops* (try SEHR uh tahps) was one of the last dinosaurs to appear. It lived in western North America about 65 million years ago. The first *Triceratops* fossils were discovered in 1887.

THE FIRST *IGUANODON*

In 1822, British amateur naturalist Mary Ann Mantell (1795-1869) found a number of **fossilized** teeth in Cuckfield, United Kingdom. Mary Ann's husband, Gideon, was a physician and a *geology* (the science of how Earth formed) enthusiast. He sent the teeth to Cuvier, hoping the French scientist would be able to identify them. Cuvier was unable to do so. He only determined that the teeth belonged to an unknown **species** (type of animal), probably a large reptile.

Mantell observed that the fossilized teeth were remarkably similar to those of an iguana. Later, he acquired additional bones and made a drawing of what he thought the animal had looked like. He called the mysterious creature an *Iguanodon* (ih GWAN uh dahn), meaning *iguana tooth*. He guessed that it might have been as long as 60 feet (18 meters). Later scientists found more complete skeletons and learned that *Iguanodons* had measured only about 30 feet (9 meters) long. In addition, Mantell had placed a bone at the animal's nose, thinking it was a horn. The more complete skeletons revealed that it was actually a bony spike that grew in the thumb location on each of the animal's hands.

By the 1840's, scientists were aware of several kinds of large, long-extinct reptiles. In 1841, British scientist Sir Richard Owen (1804-1892) suggested that these animals belonged to a group of reptiles unlike any living animals. The following year, he named the group *Dinosauria,* meaning *terribly great lizards.* Owen recognized three types of dinosaurs: Buckland's *Megalosaurus,* which in his grouping contained a **carnivore** (meat-eater), and two **herbivores** (plant-eaters)—*Iguanodon* and a

third find called *Hylaeosaurus* (hy lee uh SAWR uhs). Owen published the first major book on the reptiles of the **Mesozoic Era**. He also worked with the artist Benjamin Waterhouse Hawkins, who created a series of life-sized dinosaur sculptures in the early 1850's to display in London.

Knowledge about dinosaurs exploded in the late 1800's, as investigators discovered many enormous and surprising fossils. In 1878, miners in Bernissart, Belgium, found the first of 39 nearly complete *Iguanodon* skeletons. Louis Dollo (1857-1931) of the Royal Belgian Institute of Natural Sciences oversaw the recovery of the fossils and dedicated 40 years to studying them. He was able to unravel many of their mysteries, including the true position

FOUNDING FOSSILS

Visitors to the Natural History Museum in London can see the *Iguanodon* teeth discovered by Mary Ann Mantell in 1822. The teeth are characteristic of a plant-eating dinosaur.

IMAGINARY COMBAT

An illustration (above right) made in 1891 portrayed an imaginary fight between an *Iguanodon* and a *Megalosaurus* (at right). Scientists have since shown that these dinosaurs lived during different periods and that *Megalosaurus* walked on its two back legs.

of the "nose spike" that actually belonged on *Iguanodon's* hands.

THE BONE WARS

In the United States, the study of dinosaurs became highly competitive in the late 1800's. Two well-known American paleontologists played the leading roles in what became known as the *Bone Wars*. Edward Drinker Cope (1840-1897) from the University of Pennsylvania and Othniel Charles Marsh (1831-1899) of Yale University started out as friends, but soon became rivals as they competed over the best locations for finding fossils. Some accounts put the final break in 1870, when Cope invited Marsh to see the skeleton of a large extinct ocean reptile called a plesiosaur (PLEE see uh sawr), which he had

assembled. Marsh pointed out that Cope had reversed the direction of the *vertebrae* (bones of the spine), so the animal's head was mounted at the end of its tail. In later years, Marsh reported the story to newspapers to try to damage Cope's reputation.

The bitter rivalry of the Bone Wars proved productive for science, however. Between 1870 and 1899, teams directed and financed by Cope and Marsh uncovered tons of fossils in the western United States. They discovered well over 100 new dinosaur **species.**

The 1800's ended with the discovery in Wyoming of one of the strangest—and most popular—dinosaurs ever found. American paleontologist John Bell Hatcher (1861-1904) unearthed a creature with a short horn on its

snout and two larger horns, one above each eye. The animal measured about 25 feet (7.6 meters) long and may have weighed some 12 tons (11 metric tons). Like many other investigators of the time, Hatcher sent his fossils to Marsh for study and identification. Marsh named the animal *Triceratops*, which means *face with three horns.*

Science owes the discovery of one of the largest carnivores of the **Cretaceous Period** to the work done in Montana between 1902 and 1910 by American paleontologist Barnum Brown (1873-1963). Brown located two separate, incomplete skeletons of a new type of dinosaur. Another American paleontologist, Henry Fairfield Osborn (1857-1935), studied the finds. He named the new dinosaur *Tyrannosaurus* (tih ran uh SAWR uhs) *rex,* meaning *king of the tyrant lizards. Tyrannosaurus rex* (abbreviated as *T. rex*) lived in North America about 68 to 65 million years ago. It was one of the largest, strongest, and most ferocious **carnivores** that ever existed.

Monstrous jaws and huge claws certainly made *T. rex* look like a hunter. However, the animal measured about 40 feet (12 meters) long and its muscular body probably weighed some 7 tons (6.3 metric tons). A few paleontologists have wondered whether such a massive creature could have run fast enough to chase prey. They think *T. rex* might have been a scavenger feeding mainly on dead animals that it found. Most scientists, however, believe the dinosaur probably could manage short bursts of speed for attack runs, making it an effective hunter.

A NEW VIEW OF DINOSAURS

By the mid-1900's, hundreds of **species** of dinosaurs had been found all over the world. Then, the American *paleontologist* (scientist who studies animals, plants, and other living things from **prehistoric** times) John H. Ostrom (1928-2005) suggested an idea that revolutionized people's understanding of the animals. Ostrom claimed that dinosaurs were actually more similar to birds than to reptiles. Some early researchers had pointed out a number of physical similarities between dinosaurs and birds. In the 1860's, the British biologist Thomas Henry Huxley (1825-1895) had suggested that the similarities might mean that both had evolved from a common ancestor. However, Ostrom proposed that some dinosaurs were actually the ancestors of birds. He based the idea partly on his reexamination of *Archaeopteryx* (AHR kee OP tuhr ihks, meaning ancient wing).

This feathered animal from the **Jurassic Period** had some features in common with dinosaurs, but is now regarded as a primitive bird. Additional support for Ostrom's theory came in the late 1990's with the discovery in China of several new species of dinosaurs with wings. Specialists continue to explore unanswered questions raised by Ostrom's work. They ask which dinosaurs are most closely related to birds. They know fully modern birds existed by the end of the **Cretaceous Period** but wonder just when they first appeared.

Robert Bakker (1945-) is another paleontologist who helped change people's perception of dinosaurs. Before the 1970's, dinosaurs were thought of as slow, lumbering lizards. In his book *The Dinosaur Heresies* (1986), Bakker suggested that, unlike other reptiles, dinosaurs were warm-blooded. That means they controlled their own body temperature like **mammals** do. If dinosaurs were warm blooded, they would have eaten more food, been faster and more active, and been more likely to care for their young. Bakker's theory ushered in the "dinosaur renaissance (rebirth)" with more active portrayals of dinosaurs in art and an increased public interest in **paleontology**.

FINDS AROUND THE WORLD

Since the late 1900's, a renewed interest in paleontology, stimulated by Ostrom's findings, has contributed to the discovery of many new dinosaur species. The search for new fossils has extended all over the world. Paul Sereno (1957-), a professor at the University of Chicago and a *National Geographic* explorer, is among the paleontologists working on multiple continents. Sereno has supervised expeditions in such places as Mongolia, Morocco, and Niger.

Georges Cuvier
(1769-1832)

Naturalist and French zoologist, in his day he was the greatest authority on animal biology. He made great advances in the field of comparative **anatomy** (study of the biological structure of living things), which began a new science, paleontology. He developed the *stratigraphy* method (ordering finds by position of strata, or layers, of Earth) and identified such prehistoric animals as the *Pterodactylus* ("flying reptile") and the *Mosasaurus* ("aquatic reptile"). He created the concept of **"extinction"**— when every member of a *species* (kind) of living thing has died. He also created the term "age of the reptiles," used popularly to refer to the times of the dinosaurs. Cuvier was a follower of a scientific theory called catastrophism *(kuh TAS truh fihz uhm),* the concept that great events on Earth (including the extinction of living creatures) were due to brief catastrophic events.

FOUNDER French scientist Georges Cuvier—the founder of paleontology—is one of the most important scientists in biology.

John Ostrom
(1928-2005)

One of the main figures of the so-called "rebirth of the dinosaurs," American paleontologist John Ostrom advanced Thomas Huxley's theory (accepted today) that birds descended from the dinosaurs. He was Robert T. Bakker's mentor.

COMEBACK Besides revitalizing the study of dinosaurs in the 1960's, Ostrom discovered the dinosaur *Deinonychus.*

Othniel C. Marsh (1831-1899)

Born in the state of New York, he studied geology, mineralogy, and anatomy and was a professor at Yale University. Thanks to his efforts, philanthropist and banker George Peabody, Marsh's uncle, funded the Peabody Museum of Natural History at Yale University. Othniel Charles Marsh became the unofficial director of the institution. At the end of the 1800's, he came into competition with Edward Cope to discover dinosaur **fossils**—this competition was called the "Bone Wars." The teams led by Marsh discovered more than 500 fossil **species**, among them 80 species of dinosaurs. (Cope, for his part, discovered 56 species.) Marsh discovered and named some of the most popular dinosaurs, such as *Triceratops, Diplodocus, Allosaurus, Apatosaurus* (formerly known as *Brontosaurus), Ornithomimus,* and *Stegosaurus.* Further, he discovered the first **pterosaurs** of the United States and developed methods of **excavation** (digging) that extended to all parts of **paleontology.**

DISCOVERER Marsh's finds of dinosaurs and other animal species increased understanding of the Mesozoic Era (225 to 66 million years ago).

> *"It is not improbable that birds originated from the dinosaurs."*
> Othniel C. Marsh

Robert T. Bakker

(1945-)

Another paleontologist who changed how the public imagined dinosaurs, Bakker believes that at least some dinosaurs were endothermic (warm-blooded). The change in their behaviors based on endothermy would have been profound.

GAME-CHANGER Robert Bakker changed how we imagine dinosaurs from slow, lumbering animals, to swift, agile predators.

Mary Anning

(1799-1847)

This British scientist found and identified important fossils of prehistoric animals. She was an early leader in paleontology. But Anning received little recognition in her lifetime, largely because she was a woman.

Anning made her first major fossil discovery when she was only 12 years old. The fossil belonged to an ichthyosaur, a prehistoric marine reptile. Anning went on to find the first plesiosaur, another marine reptile. Anning made many important contributions to science. She helped to prove that many animals have become extinct. This idea was once controversial because many people held religious beliefs that life did not change over time. Anning's work helped to lay the foundation for the theory of evolution.

UNRECOGNIZED British paleontologist Mary Anning was a leader in her field who went unrecognized during her lifetime.

Footprints from the Past

Although the first fossils identified as dinosaurs came from Europe, many of the major **Mesozoic** fossil sites are on other continents. Often, these areas also contain the remains of other types of extinct creatures from other geological times.

Main fossil sites

Fossil remains of dinosaurs exist on every continent, even Antarctica. Some of the main sites are in East Africa, western Argentina, Australia, central and western China, and western North America.

Tyrannosaurus rex

The first *Tyrannosaurus rex* discovery occurred in the western United States.

Wyoming, United States

Wyoming contains a wealth of **Jurassic** fossils. Starting in the 1870's, discoveries have included *Apatosaurus* (uh PAT oh SAWR uhs) and *Diplodocus*.

The world of the dinosaurs

About 250 million years ago, Earth had a single supercontinent that scientists call Pangaea (pan JEE uh).

Permian extinction

The Permian Period (about 300 million to 250 million years ago) ended with the world's worst extinction (die off) wiping out about 95 percent of all **species**. Most scientists believe massive volcanic eruptions in what is now western Siberia led to the extinction. Dinosaurs appeared early in the following Mesozoic Era.

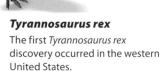

Eurasia

North America

Africa

India

South America

Antarctica

Australia

Lyme Regis, United Kingdom

Mesozoic fossils found in this region since the early 1800's include a fishlike reptile called an ichthyosaur (IHK thee uh sawr) and a type of flying **reptile** called a pterodactyl.

NORTH AMERICA

SOUTH AMERICA

Piatnitzkysaurus

Piatnitzkysaurus (pyaht NIHT skee SAWR uhs) was a large meat-eating dinosaur of the Jurassic Period. It lived in what is now Argentina.

Patagonia, Argentina

Among the many dinosaur fossils found in the region of Patagonia are those of *Carnotaurus* (kahr nuh TAWR uhs, meaning meat-eating bull) and *Patagosaurus* (PAT uh goh SAWR uhs).

Are Dinosaurs the Largest Animals Ever to Inhabit Earth?

Exact sizes can be hard to determine because of the fragmented condition of many fossils. Some dinosaur **species** appear to have reached 130 feet (40 meters) long. By comparison, the blue whale measures up to about 100 feet (30 meters) in length and can weigh over 150 tons (135 metric tons). The largest dinosaurs included *Seismosaurus* (SYZ muh sawr uhs), *Argentinosaurus* (ahr juhn TEE nuh SAWR uhs), *Supersaurus* (SOO per sawr uhs), and *Puertasaurus* (pwair tuh SAWR uhs).

Siberia, Russia

A feathered dinosaur found in Siberia in 2014, *Kulindadromeus*, caused scientists to realize that many species of dinosaurs that were not among the birdlike theropods may have had featherlike structures.

ASIA

EUROPE

Gobi Desert, China and Mongolia

Cretaceous species discovered in the Flaming Cliffs region of the Gobi Desert include *Oviraptor*, *Protoceratops* (proh toh SEHR uh tahps), and *Velociraptor*.

AFRICA

AUSTRALIA

Rukwa Rift Basin, Tanzania

In the southwestern part of the country of Tanzania, scientists discovered the skeleton of a giant titanosaur that they named *Rukwatitan* (ruhk wah TY tuhn).

Queensland, Australia

A **theropod** similar to *Velociraptor*, named *Australovenator wintonensis*, was found in the Winton Formation in Australia.

A Dinosaur Named Sue

The most complete and best-preserved *Tyrannosaurus rex* fossil in the world is called Sue. The fossil was found in 1990. After careful reconstruction, it was installed at the Field Museum in Chicago in 2000.

1

 WORLD RECORDS

Sue is about 90 percent intact, making it the most complete *Tyrannosaurus* ever found. It is also the largest known *T. rex*, measuring 42 feet (12 meters) long. Sue is the most expensive dinosaur fossil ever purchased. The museum paid about $8.4 million for it.

 UNKNOWN GENDER

Like most dinosaur fossils, Sue's gender is unknown. The name comes from its discoverer, Susan Henderson.

Gigantic Teeth

Serrated, pointed *Tyrannosaurus* teeth were well suited to a **carnivorous** diet, especially for biting and tearing flesh and bones. Their curved shape made it difficult for prey to escape. *T. rex* could bite with more force than a **crocodile**. About 58 of Sue's teeth (left) were found. They measured between 7.5 and 12 inches (19 to 30 centimeters) long.

3 **VERY OLD**

Sue lived longer than any other known *T. rex*. The bones show the dinosaur lived for 28 years. The scientists can tell the dinosaur had an infection. Its bones show calluses, fractures, and arthritis.

What Did Dinosaurs Look Like?

Scientists have worked for many years to try to figure out what dinosaurs looked like and how they lived. The task is not easy, since the only information available comes from fossil fragments.

Everything known about dinosaurs is a result of the clever but hard work of the scientists who have studied **fossil** remains of the animals. Over the years, there have been many debates about the origins, physical appearance, behavior, scientific classification, and evolution of these fascinating and mysterious creatures. New answers—and new questions—are being uncovered all the time.

ANCESTORS AND RELATIVES

Dinosaurs belonged to a group of closely related animals called *archosaurs* (AHR kuh sawrz, meaning *ruling reptiles*). Scientists believe all archosaurs were descended from small, meat-eating reptiles. These archosaur ancestors were fast-moving hunters. Some of them chased prey on their hind legs, and some ran on all four legs. Scientists have found fossils of several types of early archosaurs from the beginning of the **Mesozoic Era.**

Dinosaurs inhabited Earth for about 160 million years during the Mesozoic Era. The earliest dinosaurs appeared about 230 million years ago, during the era's Triassic Period. Most of them became extinct about 65 million years ago, at the end of the **Cretaceous**.

Dinosaurs were the dominant animals of the Mesozoic Era, but they were not the only archosaurs around at the time. Other archosaurs included **crocodilians,** the ancestors of alligators and crocodiles, and **prehistoric** flying lizards called **pterosaurs.**

DINOSAUR GROUPS

We know that dinosaurs came in lots of shapes and sizes. Many were gigantic, but some were quite small. Some were **carnivores,** but the majority were **herbivores**. For scientists, one of the most significant differences was in the structure of their hipbones.

Scientists classify true dinosaurs into two large scientific *orders* (groups): **Ornithischia** (AWR nuh THIHS kee uh) and **Saurischia** (saw RIHS kee uh). The division is based mainly on the structure of the three bones that make up the hipbone. In ornithischians, whose name means *bird-hipped*, the hipbone was tilted toward the back, as in birds. Saurischians, whose name means *lizard-hipped*, had a more upright hip structure, similar to modern reptiles. Despite these differences, all dinosaurs walked with their legs beneath them and their bellies raised off the ground, unlike modern reptiles, which walk with their legs

What Is the Role of a Paleoartist?

Science has turned to paleoartists to help portray what dinosaurs may have looked like. Paleoartists include painters, sculptors, and other artists. They reconstruct the appearance of extinct animals from the information about **anatomy** and size given to them by **paleontologists.** The results are a blend of science and art. Most representations of dinosaurs are faithful to the scientific findings provided by paleontologists. However, reliable data simply may not exist for some features, such as color or skin texture. The artists and scientists then compare the dinosaurs to modern **species** living in similar habitats and use their imaginations to fill in the missing information. As scientists make new discoveries, the artists revise their images.

Hunter and prey

A computer recreation shows a *Tyrannosaurus rex* hunting an *Ornithomimus*. Even though the *Ornithomimus* stood some 7 feet (2 meters) tall and was about 20 feet (6 meters) long, it seems small compared to the gigantic hunter. Most scientists believe *T. rex* was capable of short, fast bursts of speed, but its incredible weight prevented it from running for long distances. *Ornithomimus*, on the other hand, was one of the fastest dinosaurs. It resembled modern-day ostriches and could probably run as swiftly—30 to 40 miles (48 to 64 kilometers) per hour. It also could maintain speed longer than a *Tyrannosaurus*. Usually, it would have had a good chance of outrunning a *T. rex*.

SURPRISE ATTACK
Onithomimus could kick to defend itself, although it would have fled when facing a large predator.

sprawled to each side and their bellies on or near the ground.

There were many kinds of **ornithischians,** but all of them were plant eaters. They had a beaklike bone in front of their lower jaw. Many had bony plates in their skin for protection. They included such dinosaurs as *Stegosaurus, Iguanodon,* and *Triceratops.*

The **saurischians** are divided into two groups: **sauropodomorphs** (SAWR uh PAHD uh mawrphs) and **theropods** (THUR uh pahdz). The sauropodomorphs were plant eaters. Some late sauropodomorphs, called **sauropods,** were the giants of the

dinosaur world, reaching more than 100 feet (30 meters) in length. They included *Seismosaurus* and *Supersaurus.*

The theropods were powerful animals that walked upright on their two hind legs. Although some theropods may have been plant eaters, this group also included the only meat-eating dinosaurs. *Tyrannosaurus rex* is the best-known **carnivorous** theropod. Others include such smaller hunters as 9-foot (2.7-meter)-long *Deinonychus* (dy NON ih kuhs) and 6-foot (1.8-meter)-long *Velociraptor.* Oddly enough, even though theropods had the more reptile-like

hipbones, most scientists believe the small, meat-eating theropods were the ancestors of modern birds.

IN ALL SIZES
It is a myth that all dinosaurs were enormous. Some of them certainly were gigantic. A *Brachiosaurus* found between 1907 and 1912 in Tanzania may have stood 40 feet (12 meters) tall and could have weighed some 60 tons (54 metric tons). *Seismosaurus* was around 110 feet (33 meters) long, and *Argentinosaurus* probably weighed about 100 tons (90 metric tons). However, small dinosaurs also existed. *Microraptor* (my kroh RAP tuhr) was a

Footprints from the past

The footprints of three-toed dinosaurs have been found in the Painted Desert in Arizona. The prints, preserved in fossilized ground, came from meat-eating dinosaurs. They suggest that this type of dinosaur may have hunted in packs. In other places, evidence from dinosaur footprints has supported theories that some dinosaurs cared for their young and that some *migrated* (moved from place to place for food).

feathered dinosaur about the size of a crow. Researchers discovered it in Liaoning Province in northwestern China during the late 1990's. *Microraptor's* arms resembled wings with long feathers. Similar feathers on its back legs gave it the appearance of having four wings. Scientists believe *Microraptor* could glide between tree branches but are not sure whether it could fly.

Dinosaurs also varied greatly in their *agility* (ease of movement) and speed. Because of their enormous size, the giant sauropods would have moved very slowly. Some of the smaller theropods, such as

Deinonychus and *Velociraptor,* were fast, active predators.

WAYS OF LIFE
Many of the liveliest scientific debates about dinosaurs concern their behavior. Naturally, it is difficult to be certain about the behavior patterns of living creatures based solely on their **fossil** remains. Nevertheless, hints have survived. Fossil sites that contain many animal skeletons of the same **species** suggest that some dinosaurs lived in groups. One such site, at Bernissart, Belgium, contained the remains of more than 30 *Iguanodons.*

Ichnites (fossilized footprints) can provide clues about the way dinosaurs walked, their size and speed, and aspects of their social behavior. Scientists have developed computer models to show how dinosaurs may have moved based on footprint patterns and comparisons with modern animals, such as birds and **crocodiles,** with similar anatomies and similar roles in their environments. Ichnites found at such sites as Lark Quarry in Queensland, Australia, suggest that some types of dinosaurs lived in herds. Many dinosaurs seem to have cooperated in groups to protect their young.

Evolution in the Mesozoic Era

Dinosaurs were so successful at adapting to the environment that they dominated Earth for about 160 million years. They originated about 230 million years ago during the **Triassic Period** and disappeared at the end of the **Cretaceous Period.** Exactly why they died out is a mystery.

The family tree of dinosaurs

Dinosaurs belonged to a group of related animals called **archosaurs.** Other archosaurs included **crocodilians** and **pterosaurs.** The archosaurs probably all evolved from the same ancestors.

CROCODILIA

The ancestors of **crocodiles** had enormous evolutionary success during the **Mesozoic era** and survived the mass **extinction** of that time.

TYRANNOSAURUS REX

Tyrannosaurus rex is one of the most famous dinosaurs. It was a killing machine with smashing jaws, powerful legs, and tearing claws.

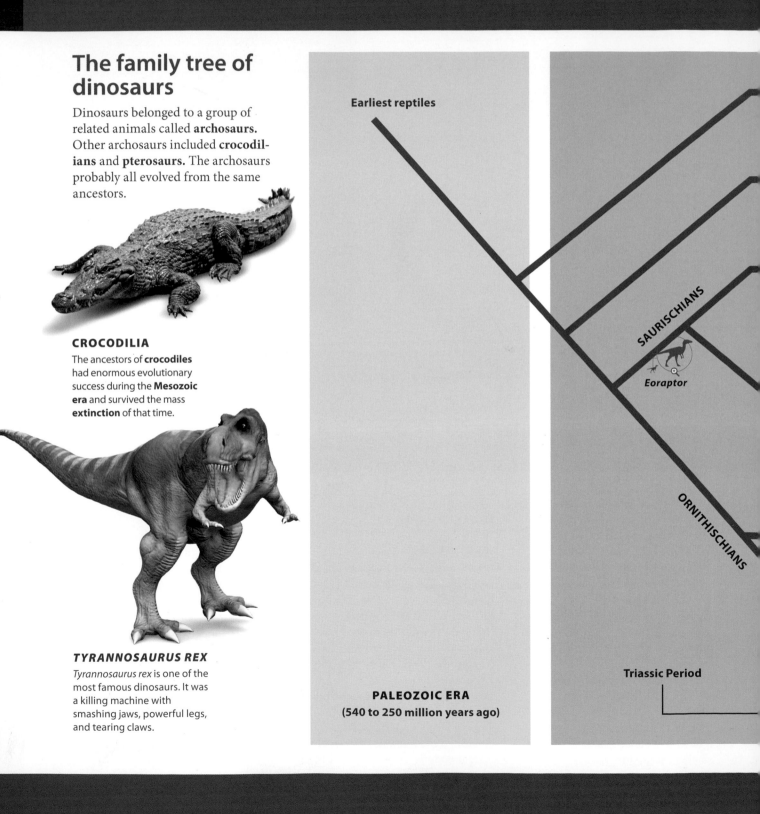

Earliest reptiles

SAURISCHIANS

Eoraptor

ORNITHISCHIANS

PALEOZOIC ERA
(540 to 250 million years ago)

Triassic Period

How Did the Bodies of Giant Sauropods Transport Blood to the Brain?

The largest dinosaurs were the **sauropods,** such as *Diplodocus*. Their necks were so long that their hearts may have had to pump with great force for blood to reach their brains. Some **paleontologists** think that the sauropods could not raise their necks too high, because that would have forced the heart to work even harder.

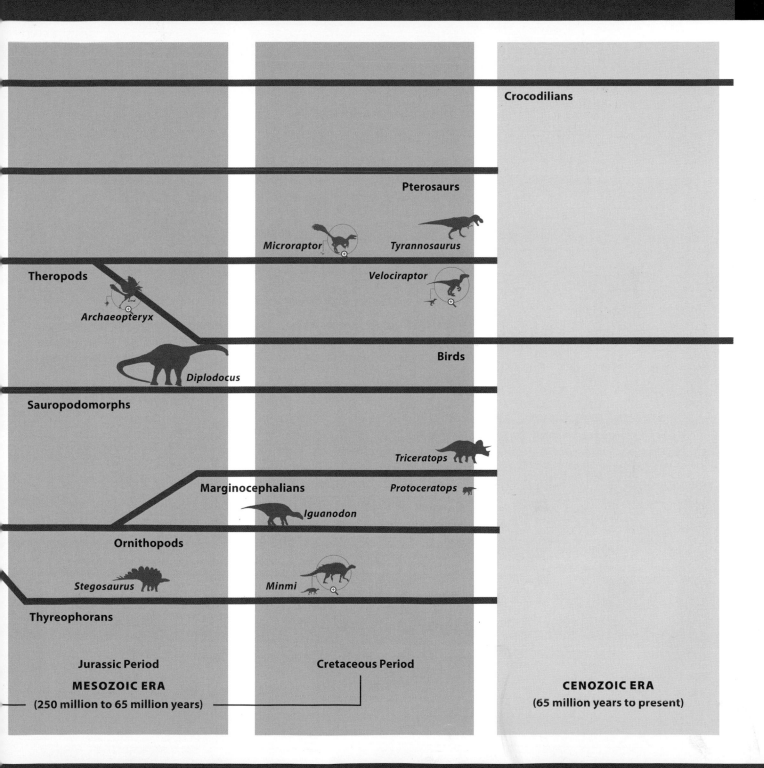

Crocodilians

Pterosaurs

Microraptor

Tyrannosaurus

Theropods

Velociraptor

Archaeopteryx

Diplodocus

Birds

Sauropodomorphs

Triceratops

Marginocephalians

Protoceratops

Iguanodon

Ornithopods

Stegosaurus

Minmi

Thyreophorans

Jurassic Period

Cretaceous Period

MESOZOIC ERA

(250 million to 65 million years)

CENOZOIC ERA

(65 million years to present)

How a Fossil Is Restored

Paleontologists use a variety of methods to reconstruct the appearance of dinosaurs. Even with the aid of computers and other technology, the task requires careful labor and may take years.

Long and delicate process

The process from finding **fossils** in the field to mounting them in a museum has many stages. Each step requires care and patience. The reconstruction process may take several years and involve specialists in many areas. The stages in the process fall into two basic phases: cleaning and assembly.

3 CLEANUP IN THE LAB

After cutting away the cast, paleontologists use fine cutting tools or a weak acid solution to remove the plain rock around the fossil. X rays and **CT scans** help them distinguish between fossil and rock.

PRECISION INSTRUMENTS

Removing fossils from rock requires delicate work with electric grinding tools.

1 FINDING THE FOSSIL

The **excavation** of a fossil requires tools ranging from small brushes to *pneumatic drills* (drills powered by compressed air).

Representations

BRONTOSAURUS EXCELSUS. Marsh. ¼

PAPER DRAWINGS

In the 1800's, Othniel C. Marsh made this drawing of a *Brontosaurus*, now known as *Apatosaurus*. Even today, drawings remain the most widely used method of illustrating the original appearance of dinosaurs.

2 PROTECTION AND TRANSPORT

Many fossils are fragile. Workers may wrap exposed sections in layers of wet cloth soaked in plaster. After this plaster cast hardens, they can safely chip the fossil out of the surrounding rock and ship it to a laboratory.

Computer Images

Paleontologist Jack Horner (1946-) reads a scan of a *Lambeosaurus* (lam bee uh SAWR uhs) skull. Computer generated imagery can create a three-dimensional picture of the inside of a body. The scan allows researchers to distinguish between the fossil and the rock that surrounds it and to determine the content of fossilized bones.

INSTRUMENTS

Tiny picks and even small needles may be used to clean the fossil.

4 CASTING THE BONES

Fossils are often too fragile to be on display. Workers use a mold of the original fossil to make a copy.

5 ASSEMBLY

Final assembly relies on scientific evidence and computer models.

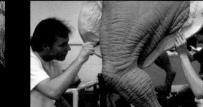

ROBOTS

Many museums illustrate how live dinosaurs probably appeared using robots or *animatronic* (electronically powered) models.

SCULPTURES

Artists work with **anatomy** experts to envision the shape of the muscles that the animals once had.

COMPUTER ANIMATION

Computer models can help reconstruct the appearance and movement patterns of animals known only by their bones.

Were They Warm-Blooded or Cold-Blooded?

Some scientists think that several dinosaurs could have been warm-blooded.

How much did a dinosaur eat? Were dinosaurs fast or sluggish? How well could they adjust to changes in weather and climate? These are just a few of the questions that might be answered by knowing whether dinosaurs were warm-blooded or cold-blooded.

The bodies of cold-blooded, or *ectothermic,* animals have little internal control over temperature. They are warm when their surroundings are warm and cool when their surroundings are cool. Cold often makes them sluggish. Modern ectothermic land animals, such as reptiles, may adjust their temperature by lying in the sun to warm up or moving into shade to cool off.

Warm-blooded, or *endothermic,* animals maintain about the same body temperature, regardless of their surroundings. This requires plenty of fuel in the form of food. Modern birds and **mammals,** both warm-blooded, may use up to 90 percent of the food they eat to maintain their body temperatures.

If dinosaurs were warm-blooded, they might have been more active and adaptive than if they were cold-blooded. But could a warm-blooded animal the size of giant *Apatosaurus* or *Tyrannosaurus* survive? How much would it have to eat? Scientists have pondered these questions for years. Until a few decades ago, most investigators thought dinosaurs must have been cold-blooded, like modern reptiles, particularly because of the large amount of food that a big endothermic dinosaur might have required.

NEW VISION

Since the 1970's, paleontologist Robert Thomas Bakker has developed a striking series of arguments to support his theory that dinosaurs were warm-blooded. He emphasized similarities between dinosaurs and today's warm-blooded animals—birds and mammals. The evidence included internal bone structure, bone chemistry, and the fact that some dinosaurs were covered with small feathers, providing insulation. He showed that, like birds, many **theropods** had a large brain and were very agile. He said the largest **sauropods** must have had very developed hearts, capable of pumping blood along their long necks to their heads. A warm-blooded animal needs a strong heart to support a *metabolic rate* (rate of burning food) higher than that of a cold-blooded animal. John Ostrom previously had pointed out that dinosaur skulls showed no sign of a *pineal eye,* a light-sensitive organ that helps regulate temperature in many cold-blooded animals.

Nevertheless, some critics objected to Bakker's conclusions. Today, most scientists believe Bakker was correct that dinosaurs were fast-moving. There are still questions being researched about warm-bloodedness.

Both types

Many paleontologists now suspect that both endothermic and ectothermic dinosaurs may have existed. They think some small theropods, similar to birds, were probably warm-blooded, but that other dinosaurs, especially the largest ones, were more likely cold-blooded with special mechanisms to help regulate body heat. Perhaps their large size slowed temperature change, helping them to maintain a more constant temperature.

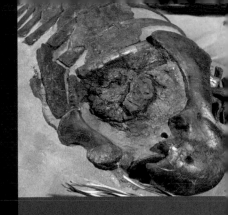

A Fossilized Dinosaur Heart—Maybe

In 1993, the remains of a *Thescelosaurus* (thehs kehl uh SAWR uhs) were found in South Dakota, in the Midwestern United States. In 2000, a description of the fossil in *Science* magazine caused a sensation. The article claimed that the remains (above) included a fossilized heart. It said the heart had four chambers and features that resembled the heart of a bird or **mammal** more than a **reptile.** If true, this would be evidence in favor of the theory that some dinosaurs were warm-blooded. Modern birds and mammals have more powerful hearts than reptiles to support their higher metabolic rates. But was the fossilized material really a heart? Many specialists doubt it. In the object's present fossilized state, a definite identification is difficult.

THESCELOSAURUS

A fossilized skull of *Thescelosaurus* helped scientists reconstruct what this plant-eating dinosaur may have looked like.

Are Birds the Descendants of Dinosaurs?

Recent fossil evidence has shown an evolutionary relationship between dinosaurs and birds. Scientists are discovering more and more support for the theory all the time, yet some puzzling findings remain unexplained.

The idea that dinosaurs and birds are somehow related is not new. In 1868, Thomas Henry Huxley claimed such a relationship existed, based on birdlike characteristics in the bone patterns of the small dinosaur *Compsognathus* (kahmp suh NAY thuhs) and in *Archaeopteryx,* the **Jurassic** animal now actually regarded as an ancient type of bird. In the 1920's, Danish paleontologist Gerhard Heilmann highlighted the extraordinary similarity between birds and **theropod** dinosaurs, even though the absence of a fork-shaped *furcula* (wishbone) in any dinosaur **fossils** had made other experts skeptical about a link. Formed by the merging of the collarbones, the furcula adds strength and flexibility where the wing muscles pull on the bones of the bird's chest. It is a fundamental part of bird **anatomy.**

Then in the late 1900's, new evidence challenged the skeptics. The furcula was found in a number of theropods, including *Oviraptor* and *Velociraptor.* Most scientists now believe that the presence of a furcula demonstrates close links between *Archaeopteryx,* some theropod dinosaurs, and modern-day birds.

SIMILAR CHARACTERISTICS

In 1973, John Ostrom published a brief but powerful article called "The Ancestry of Birds," in which he noted some 20 structural characteristics common to birds and dinosaurs. He claimed that these characteristics formed a body of convincing evidence showing that birds are direct descendants of **carnivorous** dinosaurs similar to the *Velociraptor.*

Still, not everyone is convinced. Despite mounting evidence that some theropods could have been the ancestors of birds, some specialists believe, instead, that birds and dinosaurs evolved independently from a common ancestor. Once again, anatomy is the "bone" of contention.

One problem is this: the hands of theropods generally have three fingers. The fingers correspond to what, on humans, would be the thumb and the first two fingers, and they lack the ring finger and pinky. Birds also have three fingers. In their case, however, the fingers they lack correspond to the pinky and the thumb. How could this have come about? A number of suggestions and models have been proposed, but so far the question remains unanswered.

Did Dinosaurs Protect Their Young in Nests?

It is widely known that, like present-day birds and **reptiles,** dinosaurs laid eggs with hard shells. Many fossil hunters have found dinosaur eggs.

The next question is whether dinosaurs laid their eggs and then left them, like some modern reptiles, or whether they hatched the eggs and cared for their young. Fossilized nests and hatchlings found in Montana, in the northwestern United States, in 1979 gave the first indication that the young of at least some dinosaur **species** remained in their nests under parental care after they hatched. Scientists named the nest-building species found in Montana *Maiasaura* (MAY uh sawr uh), meaning *good mother lizard*.

In 1993, scientists in Mongolia, in east-central Asia, discovered the skeleton of an *Oviraptor* (oh vuh RAP tuhr) in a position similar to a hen sitting on its eggs. The name *Oviraptor* means *egg thief*. Earlier finds of this dinosaur near eggs had led researchers to think it ate eggs. The new evidence completely changed the dinosaur's image.

FIRST BIRD
A fossil of *Archaeopteryx* reveals body features that seem to link the animal to both reptiles and birds.

Is It Possible to Bring the Dinosaurs Back?

Science fiction writers have imagined cloning living, breathing dinosaurs from preserved DNA. Could dinosaurs return to Earth in this way?

In his 1990 novel *Jurassic Park,* American author Michael Crichton (1942-2008) suggested a method for bringing dinosaurs to life by recovering the genetic material contained in blood cells from a dinosaur. Each living cell in a body contains a full set of the *genes*—basic units of heredity, made up of **DNA** (deoxyribonucleic acid) molecules—that determine all the hereditary characteristics of that organism. The novel, made into a successful film in 1993, drew its inspiration from experiments using the hereditary material of a living animal to try to produce another genetically identical animal, or clone, in a laboratory.

When Crichton wrote his book, scientists had already cloned some simple animals. In 1996, they were able to clone a sheep. Other cloned animals now include mice, dogs, and bulls. The success of these experiments raised the possibility of cloning recently extinct animals. In 2009, a team of French and Spanish scientists cloned a Pyrenean ibex, a type of mountain goat that had become extinct in 2000. The team used stored genetic material that had been taken from one of the last ibexes before it died. Unfortunately, the ibex clone died only minutes after birth because of a lung defect.

SOFT TISSUES

Could advances in genetic engineering enable scientists to clone an animal that went extinct in the past using DNA from a long dead animal? This would be a far more complex challenge. Muscle, fat, and even the living, growing soft tissue in bones decay quickly after death. After 65 million years (or more), the complex DNA molecules that lie within the cells of soft tissue have not survived intact.

In 2007, the American paleontologist Mary Higby Schweitzer discovered tiny bits of soft tissue that were the remnants of blood vessels inside the bone of a *Tyrannosaurus rex.* This was a startling find. No DNA survived, but she did find bits of protein. Her discoveries do not make the idea of cloning a dinosaur any more likely, but they have opened brand new windows into the past. The bits of collagen (connective tissue, which holds the body together) protein inside the *T. rex* bones have proven to be similar to that of such modern birds as chickens and ostriches.

Prehistoric Tick

The discovery of a 90-million-year-old fossilized tick locked in a piece of *amber* (fossilized resin, such as chiefly comes from pine trees) excited researchers when the find occurred in New Jersey, on the Atlantic Coast of the United States, in the 1990's. Scientists decided that the world's only **Mesozoic Era** tick should be preserved intact.

Another brief flurry of excitement occurred in 1995, when Chinese scientists, led by molecular biologist Chen Zhangliang and paleontologist Zhang Yun, announced that they had extracted fragments of DNA from a dinosaur egg. Later studies were not able to confirm their results. Many experts believe the genetic material they found was probably due to contamination of the test sample.

GENETIC EXAMINATION
A molecular biologist studies a dinosaur egg (below).

Is Cloning Something Out of Science Fiction?

The *Jurassic Park* films (above) were science fiction stories in which scientists cloned **prehistoric** reptiles using dinosaur blood taken from mosquitoes preserved in amber for millions of years. Real scientists may daydream about the chance to see and study a cloned dinosaur, but they cannot help but recognize a number of scientific flaws in the movies. For example, each mosquito would have to contain blood from just one **species** of dinosaur. The "dino DNA" would have to be preserved intact and somehow remain uncontaminated by any of the mosquito's own DNA. Also, the scientists would need a compatible egg in which to place the DNA.

On the other hand, Mary Higby Schweitzer has shown that dinosaur bones still contain startling surprises. In addition to finding dinosaur proteins, she determined that the *T. rex* she was studying was female and had been pregnant when it died.

The Tragic End of an Era

The *catastrophe* (widespread and extraordinary disaster) that ended the age of the dinosaurs must have left a scene of devastation. The catastrophe made no distinction between large or small dinosaurs. No continent on the planet remained safe. Dinosaurs became a thing of the past, leaving only one type of descendants—birds.

Catastrophe

Whether it resulted from the impact of an **asteroid** from outer space, volcanic eruptions at the Deccan Traps in India, or a combination of causes, the catastrophe ended the **Mesozoic Era.** It produced one of the greatest **extinctions** in Earth's history. About 75 percent of the animal **species** alive at the time disappeared.

FATALITIES
The great *Triceratops* of North America was among the victims of this catastrophic event. Paleontologists have found sites where hundreds of *Triceratops* died.

A Glimpse of Color

It may never be possible to know the color or skin texture of most dinosaurs. In a few cases, however, an impression revealing the texture of a dinosaur's skin remained fixed in fossilized stone (left). In 2010, scientists isolated melanosomes in the fossil feathers of a dinosaur. *Melanosomes* are *pigment- (color-) bearing* structures in a cell.

CLOUDY SKIES

Many scientists believe that the collision of a huge asteroid with Earth produced thick clouds of ash and dust that darkened the planet's skies for months or even years. Without enough sunlight, many plants died. Without plants to eat, animals died. Toxic gases also clogged the air. A huge volcanic eruption over a long period of time would have had similar effects. The volcanoes at the Deccan Traps began erupting about 250,000 years before the extinction of the dinosaurs and continued for about 500,000 years after.

A HUGE BURIAL GROUND

The extinction at the end of the Mesozoic Era turned areas of Earth's surface into huge burial grounds. In some places, the animal remains were preserved in the form of **fossils**.

When Did Dinosaurs Become Extinct?

The generally accepted theory is that the impact of a giant asteroid near the end of the Cretaceous Period caused the extinction of the majority of dinosaurs. Some scientists still wonder whether this extinction was rapid or gradual.

In the late 1970's, the Nobel prize-winning American physicist Luis Walter Alvarez (1911-1988) and his son, the **geologist** Walter Alvarez (1940-), were doing research together in Italy. They discovered an increased level of the element iridium in a narrow *stratum* (layer) of rock that corresponded to the end of the **Cretaceous Period** about 65 million years ago. Iridium is one of the rarest metals in Earth's crust, but it is abundant in **asteroids** and meteorites. The father-and-son team theorized that this high level of iridium was the result of a giant asteroid colliding with Earth. Since then, this iridium-rich layer of rock dating to 65 million years ago has been found in many locations around the planet.

In 1990, geologists identified a huge crater about 112 miles (180 kilometers) across at Chicxulub (cheek shoo lub) in Mexico. Evidence indicates that it was caused by an asteroid at least 6 miles (10 kilometers) wide striking Earth about 65 million years ago. Scientists believe this asteroid strike could have produced the iridium layer.

The asteroid impact would have thrown billions of tons of dust and debris into the atmosphere. Clouds of smoke and debris would have blocked the sun's light for months or even years. Without enough sunlight, plants died and many animals starved. In addition, the darkened skies caused temperatures to drop. Some 75 percent of all animal **species** became extinct.

ADDITIONAL CAUSES?

In 1997, scientists found evidence of a giant crater beneath the Indian Ocean. Larger than the crater at Chicxulub, it may have been made by an asteroid strike about 300,000 years later. Could a one-two asteroid punch have wiped out the dinosaurs? Other investigators believe that huge volcanic eruptions in India at the end of the Cretaceous Period were the main cause for the mass **extinction**. Some experts think the combination of blows from several catastrophic events along with significant climate and environmental changes gradually killed more and more animals and finally brought the age of the dinosaurs to an end.

SURVIVORS

Some animals survived the mass **extinction** at the end of the Cretaceous Period. They included small **mammal**s and birds protected from the cold by fur or feathers. These animals could feed on seeds, nuts, and rotting vegetation until plant life recovered. Other survivors may have escaped by burrowing in the ground or hiding at the bottom of lakes. In fact, experts now believe that not all dinosaurs became extinct at the end of the Cretaceous Period. Most scientists consider birds to be living dinosaurs that survived.

What Is the K-T Boundary?

Luis Walter Alvarez and his son Walter discovered the thin geological band known as the K-T Boundary. The events that produced the band are of great importance to Earth's history. This narrow, iridium-rich layer marks the boundary between the **Mesozoic** and Cenozoic eras. The Cenozoic is the era of geologic time that continues to the present day. The name *K-T Boundary* comes from the words *Kreidezeit,* the German spelling of Cretaceous, and *Tertiary,* an old name for what is now called the Paleogene Period at the start of the Cenozoic Era. All dinosaur **fossils** have been found in rock beneath the K-T Boundary.

SEPARATION OF ERAS
In these exposed layers of rock located in Italy, the K-T Boundary appears as a thin, dark layer.

The Volcanic Theory and the Deccan Traps

The two major theories for the cause of the mass extinction at the end of the Cretaceous Period involve 1) an asteroid strike and 2) large volcanic eruptions. The Deccan Traps are a huge lava bed in India produced by massive volcanic eruptions at the end of the Cretaceous Period. They cover about 200,000 square miles (500,000 square kilometers). In some places, they are more than 1 mile (1.6 kilometers) thick. The eruptions that deposited this material could have released huge volumes of gas that caused rapid climate change.

Some small mammals and birds were able to survive the new, colder conditions, but the large dinosaurs and reptiles became extinct. Some reptiles that were not dinosaurs also survived the extinction. These included crocodiles and sea turtles. However, the dinosaurs themselves left only one group of descendants—birds.

Reptiles ceased to be the dominant group of species, as they had been throughout the **Mesozoic Era.**

EXPANSIVE WAVE
The asteroid that struck at Chicxulub formed an enormous crater.

Gallery of Dinosaurs

The best known dinosaurs are the giants, such as *Apatosaurus* and *Tyrannosaurus rex*. However, dinosaurs came in many shapes and sizes. Here are just a few of them.

Archaeopteryx

Many scientists consider *Archaeopteryx*, whose name means ancient wing, to be the earliest known bird. The small animal lived about 150 million years ago and represents an important link in the evolution of dinosaurs into birds. Its skeleton and tail closely resembled those of a small dinosaur, but it also had feathers and birdlike wings. Based on the structure of the wings, scientists believe the animal could skillfully glide between branches. They think it could probably fly, but they are not sure how well.

The first *Archaeopteryx* fossil was discovered in 1861 and is on display at the Natural History Museum in London. The best-preserved specimen (right) was discovered in southern Germany in 1877 and is now at the Museum of Natural History in Berlin. The fossil clearly preserves the impression of wing feathers.

VELOCIRAPTOR
This feathered meat-eater lived in what are now Mongolia and northern China some 80 million years ago. It grew to about 6 feet (1.8 meters) long.

ANKYLOSAURUS
Ankylosaurus (ang kuh luh SAWR uhs), meaning *fused lizard*, describes the animal's armor of bony pieces grown together. The tail ends in a bony club. This animal lived between 68 and 65 million years ago in what is now western North America.

TRICERATOPS
Triceratops reached about 25 feet (7.6 meters) long and weighed about 8 tons (7.3 metric tons). *Triceratops* wandered what is now the western United States about 65 million years ago.

Diplodocus

This highly recognizable plant-eating dinosaur had short, heavy legs and an extremely long neck and tail. The neck alone contained 15 large vertebrae and was about 26 feet (8 meters) long. It was so long that *Diplodocus* probably could not raise its head much above its shoulders. The entire animal stretched about 90 feet (27 meters) from nose to tail, and one species of *Diplodocus* may have reached 115 feet (35 meters). It lived in what is now the western United States about 150 million years ago, near the end of the **Jurassic Period.**

Parasaurolophus

Parasaurolophus (pair uh sawr uh LAHF uhs) belonged to a group of plant-eating dinosaurs known as **hadrosaurs,** which had flattened snouts resembling duck bills. It grew to about 35 feet (10 meters) long. It had a large, bony crest on its head. This strange crest was hollow and could be as long as 6.5 feet (2 meters). Nobody knows the purpose of the crest, but some scientists think that it might have made sounds louder. This animal lived between 77 and 71 million years ago in what today is western North America.

MONOLOPHOSAURUS

One of the fiercest carnivores, *Monolophosaurus* (mahn uh lahf uh SAWR uhs) lived some 150 million years ago, at the end of the **Jurassic Period.** It had a large crest running down the center of its nose. It was first discovered in China in the 1980's.

STEGOSAURUS

A North American plant-eater, *Stegosaurus* is known for the two rows of bony plates running down its back and tail. It lived some 150 million years ago.

EORAPTOR

Scientists consider *Eoraptor* to be one of the first dinosaurs. It lived about 230 million years ago in the **Triassic Period.** The small hunter walked on two legs and was about 3 feet (9 meters) long. Its fossils were discovered in Argentina.

PARASAUROLOPHUS

Visitors to the Midland Provincial Park in Alberta, Canada, can see a large *Parasaurolophus* skeleton. This dinosaur could walk on two legs or four legs. It lived between 77 and 71 million years ago. The crest on its head could be more than 3 feet (1 meter) long. A **herbivore**, the animal lived in what today is western North America.

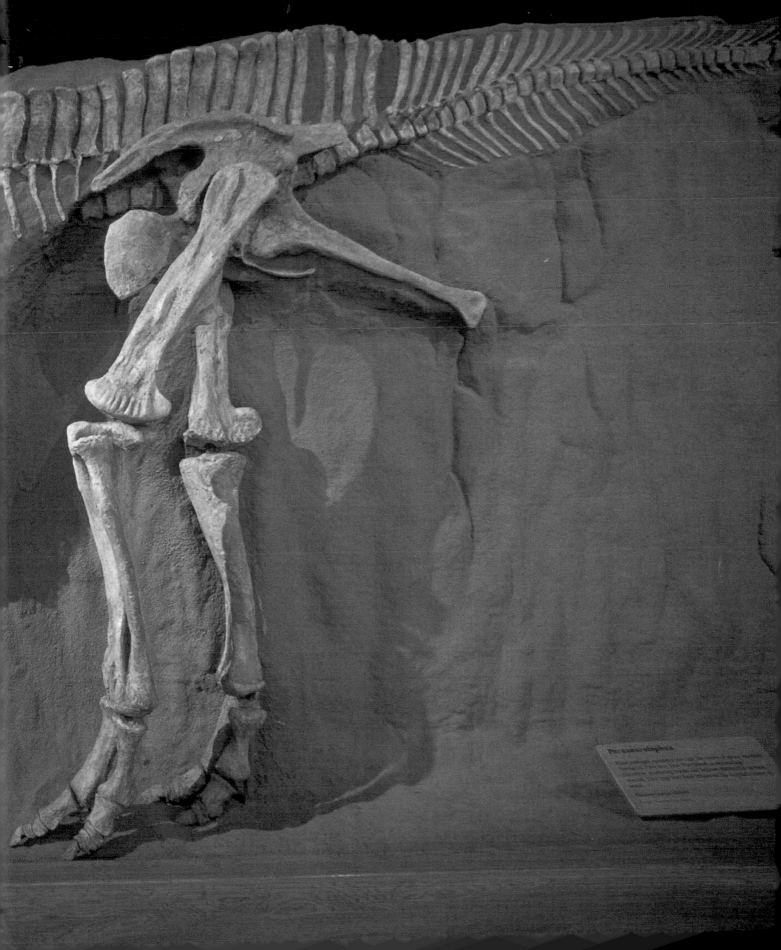

Places to See and Visit

OTHER PLACES OF INTEREST

DINOSAUR NATIONAL MONUMENT
COLORADO / UTAH, U.S.

The national monument covers about 330 square miles (850 square kilometers). In 2010, a new plant-eating dinosaur **species** called *Abydosaurus* (ah bih doh SAUR uhs) was found there. The visitors' center features a rock wall containing about 1,500 fossils.

FIELD MUSEUM
ILLINOIS, U.S.

The Field Museum in Chicago, Illinois, is one of the world's largest natural history museums. The highlight of the museum's dinosaur collection is Sue, the largest and most complete *Tyrannosaurus rex* ever found.

MUSEUM OF NATURAL HISTORY
BERLIN, GERMANY

This famous institution, also known as the Humboldt Museum, was established in 1810. It features an enormous reconstructed *Giraffatitan* (juh RAF uh ty tuhn) from the African nation of Tanzania and a fabulous *Diplodocus* skeleton 89 feet (27 meters) in length. The museum's collection also includes the world's best-preserved *Archaeopteryx* specimen.

Alberta

DINOSAUR PROVINCIAL PARK

The park covers about 30 square miles (80 square kilometers) and was established in 1955 to protect one of the most extensive dinosaur fields in the world. Hundreds of specimens, including more than 150 complete skeletons from many different species, have been found. In 1979, the park was declared a UNESCO World Heritage Site.

DEVIL'S COULEE DINOSAUR AND HERITAGE MUSEUM

Located in Warner, about 175 miles (282 kilometers) from Calgary, the museum features several exhibits detailing how dinosaur eggs were incubated and is one of the museum's star exhibits.

Royal Tyrrell Museum

The Royal Tyrrell Museum is famous for its collection of more than 130,000 fossils. It has a large collection of complete dinosaur skeletons, including a *Tyrannosaurus rex*. Visitors may also observe scientists at work on fossils. The museum is located near Drumheller, in Midland Provincial Park, about 80 miles (130 kilometers) from the provincial capital of Calgary.

NATIONAL DINOSAUR MUSEUM
CANBERRA, AUSTRALIA

The museum's exhibits take visitors on a journey through Earth's history. Displays include skeletons and models of dinosaurs from Australia and other parts of the world, as well as fossils of other plants and animals.

NATURAL HISTORY MUSEUM
LONDON, U.K.

The museum is one of the most important of its kind, housing about 70 million specimens. The **paleontology** room displays a *Diplodocus* skeleton 105 feet (32 meters) in length, and a life-sized *Tyrannosaurus* robot.

ROCKY MOUNTAIN DINOSAUR RESOURCE CENTER
COLORADO, U.S.

The center contains many fossil skeletons and sculptures illustrating the appearance of dinosaurs. Displays also feature other **prehistoric** animals, such as **pterosaurs** and plesiosaurs. A working paleontology laboratory is part of the tour.

WYOMING DINOSAUR CENTER
WYOMING, U.S.

Visitors may accompany a paleontologist to a nearby fossil dig site. *Diplodocus, Allosaurus, Camarasaurus* (kuh MAIR uh sawr uhs), and other fossils have been found in the area. The museum's gallery displays many dinosaur reconstructions, including a *Supersaurus* that is 105 feet (32 meters) long.

Glossary

Anatomy — Body structure, or the study of the biological structure of bodies.

Archosaur — A group of related animals that included crocodilians, dinosaurs, and pterosaurs.

Asteroid — A natural object that orbits a star and is smaller than a planet.

Carnivore — Any animal that eats chiefly other animals.

Cretaceous Period — The last of the three periods in the Mesozoic Era. It lasted from about 145 million to 65 million years ago.

Crocodilian —A group of reptile species that includes modern alligators, caimans, crocodiles, and gavials.

CT scan — CT, or Computed Tomography, is a system for taking X-ray pictures from multiple angles to produce three-dimensional images.

DNA — A thin, chainlike molecule that directs the formation, growth, and reproduction of cells and living things. Every living cell on Earth has DNA.

Excavation — A site where scientists dig up ancient objects, such as fossils.

Extinction — When every member of a species of living things has died.

Fossil — The preserved mark or remains of a living thing from long ago.

Geologist — A scientist who studies how Earth formed and changed.

Hadrosaur —A diverse group of dinosaurs with wide snouts resembling duck bills.

Herbivore — Any animal that eats chiefly plants.

Ichnite — Fossilized footprint.

Jurassic Period — The middle of the three periods in the Mesozoic Era. It lasted from about 200 million to 145 million years ago.

Mammal — A warm-blooded animal that is born from its mother's body rather than hatched from an egg, and that feeds its young on the mother's milk.

Mesozoic Era — A long period in Earth's history, lasting from about 250 to 65 million years ago. It lay between the Paleozoic Era (about 540 to 250 million years ago) and the Cenozoic Era (about 65 million years ago to the present).

Order — A large scientific group of living or once-living things that are alike in some way.

Ornithischians — Dinosaurs of the order Ornithischia, having a bird-like hip structure.

Paleontology — The study of animals, plants, and other things that lived in prehistoric times.

Prehistoric — Long past times before written history.

Pterosaur — An extinct group of prehistoric flying reptiles.

Reptile — A scaly-skinned animal that hatches from a hard-shelled egg.

Saurischians — Dinosaurs of the order Saurischia, having a hip formation similar to lizards.

Sauropod —Later sauropodomorphs; the group includes the largest dinosaur species.

Sauropodomorph — One of the two groups of saurischian (lizard-hipped) dinosaurs.

Species — A scientific group of all the living organisms of the same kind.

Theropod — One of the two groups of saurischian (lizard-hipped) dinosaurs, it includes the only meat-eating dinosaurs.

Triassic Period — The first of the three periods in the Mesozoic Era. It lasted from about 250 to 200 million years ago.

For Further Information

Books

Dinosaurs: A Visual Encyclopedia. New York: DK Pub.,
    2013. Print.

Dixon, Dougal. *The Complete Book of Dinosaurs*. London:
    Southwater, 2012. Print.

Green, Dan, and Simon Basher. *Dinosaurs*. New York:
    Kingfisher, 2012. Print.

Paul, Gregory S. *The Princeton Field Guide to Dinosaurs*.
    Princeton, NJ: Princeton UP, 2010. Print.

Thimmesh, Catherine. *Scaly Spotted Feathered Frilled:
    How Do We Know What Dinosaurs Really Looked Like?*
    Boston: Houghton Mifflin Harcourt, 2013. Print.

Websites

"Dinosaurs." *BBC Nature*. BBC, 12 Aug. 2014. Web.
    25 Feb. 2015.

"Prehistoric Animals, Dinosaurs." *National Geographic*.
    National Geographic, 2015. Web. 25 Feb. 2015.

Stone, Richard. "Dinosaurs' Living Descendants."
    Smithsonian.com. Smithsonian, Dec. 2010. Web.
    25 Feb. 2015.

"Why Did the Dinosaurs Die Out?" *History.com*. A&E
    Television Networks, 2010. Web. 17 Feb. 2015.

Index